LOW G TUNING FOR THE UKULELE

by Dick Sheridan

To access audio visit:
www.halleonard.com/mylibrary

Enter Code
7116-9377-7781-3328

ISBN 978-1-57424-399-4
SAN 683-8022

Cover by James Creative Group

Copyright © 2020 CENTERSTREAM Publishing
P.O. Box 17878 - Anaheim Hills, CA 92817

www.centerstream-usa.com | centerstrm@aol.com | 714-779-9390

DEDICATION

"Friendship, friendship
What a perfect blendship"

To Bill Hider who introduced me to Low G tuning.
and
Doug Collingwood who provided the instrument that
made all these Low G songs come to life.

TABLE OF CONTENTS

A WORD FROM THE AUTHOR
Dick Sheridan

Despite having played the ukulele from the time I was in my early teens – and despite having written over 20 books for the uke – it was only recently that I discovered Low G tuning.

The introduction came when a friend stopped by with his concert-size ukulele and we began jamming some songs. I noticed that his uke had a much richer sound than mine. Puzzled at first, the mystery was solved when I discovered that its low 4th string was tuned down an octave from the standard "high g" tuning of gCEA.

He had replaced the usual nylon 4th string with a wound one that had a gauge of .030. I couldn't wait to try it out for myself and when I did from that moment on I was hooked. With the generous donation from another friend of a tenor-sized uke, I replaced the 4th string and a new world opened up of fun ukulele playing.

I soon realized that there was more to this new tuning than its deep resonance: it expanded the instrument's range five notes below standard tuning.

Often in putting songs together for the uke in gCEA tuning limitations of range would force me to play some notes an octave higher or lower than they should be – or even to change the melody. This might require having to transpose the song into a key that would fit the ukulele's range but was not the key of preference for singing, playing with other instruments, or for some other reason.

When arranging songs in gCEA it is not uncommon to find that the melody falls on the upper high frets of the 1st string. This can hamper the ease of playing. Trying to find a better key to lower the song isn't always easy since the range of many songs extends beyond the bottom notes of the ukulele. But with Low G tuning that range can often be extended and transposition made possible.

For example, arranging the Mexican song Cielito Lindo in the key of C places several notes in the chorus up to the 8th fret of the 1st string. But by dropping the low 4th string to G and changing the key to G, the high fret notes are now eliminated and the song fits perfectly within the uke's range.

Note: Cielito Lindo is included in the songs of the following collection.

An added attraction of this new tuning is the sound created when playing with other ukes tuned to the standard well-known "my dog has fleas." A new dimension of wider tone color emerges. Take turns alternating between melody and chords: one instrument in standard tuning plays the melody, the other in Low G plays the chords, then vice versa. Play with instruments other than the ukulele. I often accompany bluegrass banjo players with the uke especially in Low G tuning for a full sound.

If no other instrument is available to play along with, use the online audio that comes with this book. Press the Loop A box at the beginning of the song and it will repeat as often as you like.

Although you can individually replace the standard 4th string with a thicker string of your own choosing, there are several manufacturers such as D'Addario and Aquila who offer string sets dedicated to Low G as well as individual 4th strings in a choice of wound, nylon or some composite material. If you select the replacement string yourself try to stay in the range of .028 to .032. Online tuners are available to help you with pitch.

By the way, Low G tuning is sometimes referred to as "linear" meaning that the strings are aligned in a straight ascending line G-C-E-A unlike the standard sequence that jumps from a high g to a lower C-E-A.

Now having said all this in defense of Low G tuning, there is certainly no reason to abandon traditional standard tuning. It has a beauty of its own. But for variety and a fresh new sound that's exciting and different, Low G is certainly worth looking into. Try it, see for yourself. The choice is yours.

~

For a previous book in Low G tuning, check out Centerstream's "The Low G String Tuning Ukulele" (00001534).

A PRETTY GIRL
IS LIKE A MELODY

Ukulele in Low G tuning: GCEA

Irving Berlin

♩–130

D7 G7

A pret-ty girl _____ is like a mel-o-dy _____ that

CM7 C Cdim7 C

haunts you night and day _____

C67 F Fm C

just like the strain of a haunt-ing re-frain, she'll

D7 G7

start up-on a mar-a-thon and run a-round your brain. You can't es-

AFTER YOU'VE GONE

Ukulele in Low G tuning: GCEA

Henry Creamer

After you've gone and left me cry-in', af-ter you've gone there's no de-ny-in',

you'll feel blue, you'll feel sad,— you'll miss the dear-est pal you've ev-er had.—

There'll come a time, now don't for-get it, there'll come a time when you'll re-gret it

Some-day, when you grow lone - ly your heart will break like mine and you'll want me on - ly,

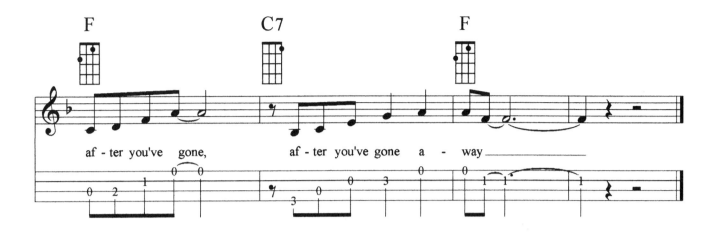

af - ter you've gone, af - ter you've gone a - way

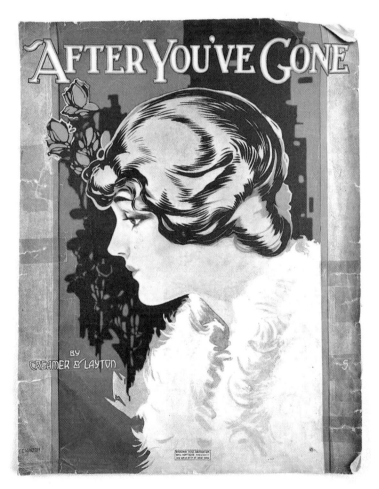

circa 1918

ALL BY MYSELF

Ukulele in Low G tuning: GCEA

Irving Berlin

ALL BY MYSELF

APRIL SHOWERS

B.G. DeSylva Ukulele in Low G tuning: GCEA Louis Silvers

CAN'T YOU HEAR ME CALLING, CAROLINE

William Henry Gardner   Ukulele in Low G tuning: GCEA   Caro Roma

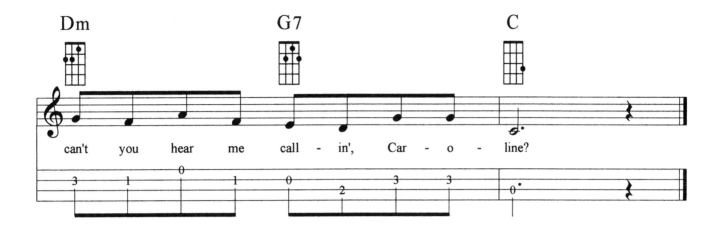

Joe Donahue was a big Irish-American cop who came to me for banjo lessons. He wanted to learn to play so he could go in to nursing homes and assisted living facilities to perform for the residents. Only problem was that his hands were large and the fingers like fat sausages. Squeezing those fingers into the tight spaces of chords and frets was impossible. But Joe was highly motivated so we devised a system where we tuned the banjo to an open chord. Then, by barring one finger across all the strings and moving up and down on the fingerboard, different chords could be sounded. Admittedly, the system had some limitations but it was good enough for Joe.

I asked Joe what songs he would particularly like to learn. His first choice was "Can't You Hear Me Callin', Caroline." The song was new to me, circa 1914, and we both worked it up together. It's now become one of my favorites.

Joe is no longer with us. But to the best of my understanding he accomplished his goal. I'm sure many a residential home resounded wth his enthusiastic strumming and responded to that generous, giving Irish heart.

circa 1914

CAROLINA IN THE MORNING

Gus Kahn   Ukulele in Low G tuning: GCEA   Walter Donaldson

G   GM7   G6   Ddim7   D7

♩=110

Noth-ing could be fin - er than to be in Car - o - lin - a in the morn - - ing,

Am   Am/Ab   Am7   D7   Gdim7   G

noth-ing could be sweet - er than my sweet - ie when I meet her in the morn - - ing,

C   G   C   E7

Where the morn - ing glor - ies twine a - round the door

A7   D   B7   Em   A7   D7

whis - per - ing pret - ty sto - ries___ I long to hear once more.

16

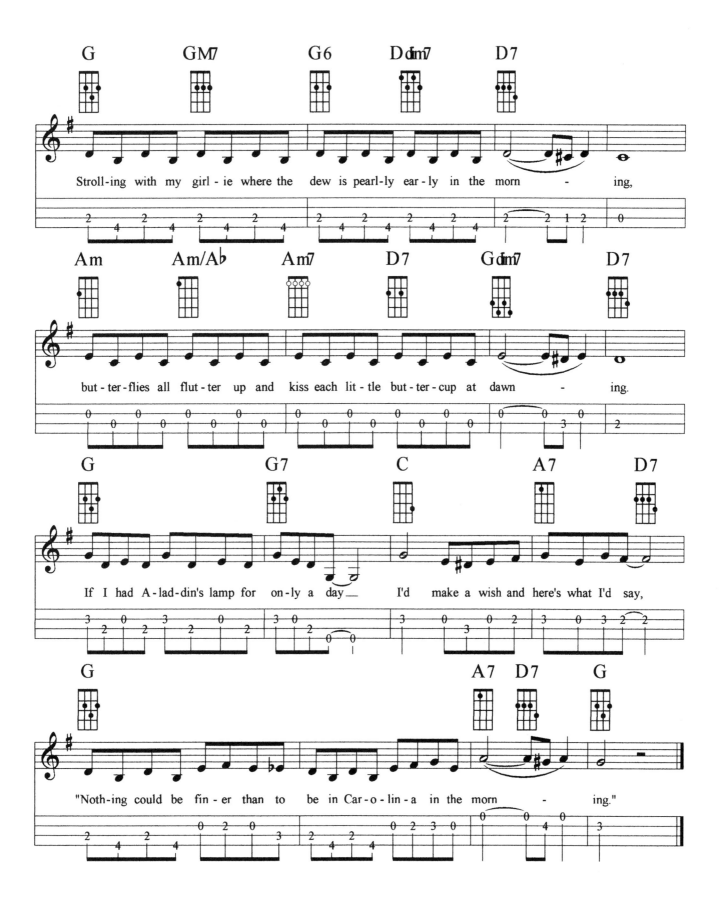

CHICAGO

Fred Fisher

Ukulele in Low G tuning: GCEA

CHICAGO

NOTE: Billy Sunday, a former professional baseball player, was a popular evangelist in Chicago in the early 1900s. He rallied against the evils of the city, especially liquor, and was a strong supporter of prohibition.

BABY, WON'T YOU PLEASE COME HOME

Ukulele in Low G tuning: GCEA

Clarence Williams & Charles Warfield

CHOPIN

Ukulele in Low G tuning: GCEA

Richard P. Sheridan

21

CIELITO LINDO

Ukulele in Low G tuning: GCEA

Traditional

DRINK TO ME ONLY WITH THINE EYES

Ukulele in Low G tuning: GCEA

Words by Ben Johnson

Traditional Melody

GYPSY LOVE SONG

Harry B. Smith Ukulele in Low G tuning: GCEA Victor Herbert

Slum-ber on, my lit-tle gyp-sy sweet-heart, dream of the field and the grove,

Can you hear me, hear me in that dream-land, where your fan-cies rove?

Slum-ber on, my lit-tle gyp-sy sweet-heart, wild lit-tle wood-land dove!

Can you hear the song that __ tells you all my __ heart's true love?

24

HELLO! MA BABY

I WANT A GIRL

Just Like The Girl That Married Dear Old Dad

William Dillon   Ukulele Low G tuning: GCEA   Harry Von Tilzer

I'M ALWAYS CHASING RAINBOWS

Joseph McCarthy Ukulele in Low G tuning: GCEA Harry Carroll

I'M ALWAYS CHASING RAINBOWS

The lovely melody of this song from 1917 was adopted from the composition
"Fantasie-Impromptu" by Frederic Chopin.

THE LOVE-SICK BLUES

Ukulele in Low G tuning: GCEA

Cliff Friend
Irving Mills

MOTHER MACHREE

Ukulele in Low G tuning: GCEA

Rida Johnson Young

Ernest R. Ball & Chauncey Olcott

John McCormack, one of the most celebrated singers of his day, introduced the song in the 1910 show "Barry Of Baltimore." In addition to McCormack, the song was favored by a long list of so-called Irish tenors including such notables as Dennis Dey,who was often featured on the Jack Benny radio shows of the 1940s, Frank Parker of the Arthur Godfrey radio and TV series, and more recently the late Irish-born Frank Patterson.

Sentimental songs of the "old country" were particularly popular in the early 1900s with the wave of immigrants, and those with Irish ancestry were especially well represented. It is interesting that many of the "Irish" songs -- just as often sung today as when first written -- were composed by American songwriters like Olcott and Ball who also collaborated on *When Irish Eyes Are Smiling.*

Mother Machree became the title of a 1929 silent movie and the song was included in the 1939 film "Rose of Washington Square." Note that the song *Rose of Washington Square* is included in this book.

Machree, by the way, is not Mother's last name. It is am adaptation from the Irish language "mo chroi" -- a term of endearment meaning "my heart."

circa 1910

MY EVALINE

Barbershop Quartet Favorite

Ukulele: Low G tuning: GCEA

Oh, Ev-a - line, ___ say you'll be mine, won't you come and let me whis-per in your ear?

Way down yon - der in the old corn field for you I've pined.

Sweet - er than the hon - ey to the hon - ey bee, I love you say

you love me. Meet me in the shade of the old ap - ple tree, ___

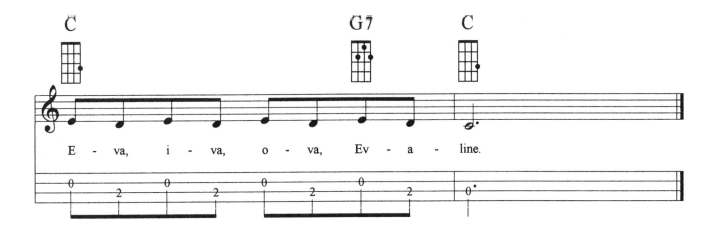

E - va, i - va, o - va, Ev - a - line.

When I was in college singing with the glee club we'd travel to different concert locations by bus always being cautioned not to sing before the concert but to save our voices. After the concert on the way back to campus it was a different matter and youthful exuberence couldn't be contained. We loved to harmonize, and the bus rang with spontaneous singing. *My Evaline* was on the top of the list.

Here's how we sang it:

> Oh, Evaline (Oh, Evaline)
> Say you'll be mine (say you'll be mine)
> Won't you come and let me whisper in your ear (your ear)
> Way down yonder in the old cornfield for you (for you) I've pined (I've pined)
> Sweeter than the honey to the honey bee
> I love you say you love me
> Meet me in the shade of the old apple tree, oh
> Eva-Iva-Ova, Eva-Iva-Ova, Eva-Iva-Ova
> Evaline

MY HONEY'S LOVIN' ARMS

Ukulele in Low G tuning: GCEA

Herman Ruby

Joseph Meyer

OH! YOU BEAUTIFUL DOLL

Seymour Brown

Ukulele Low G tuning: GCEA

Nat D Ayer

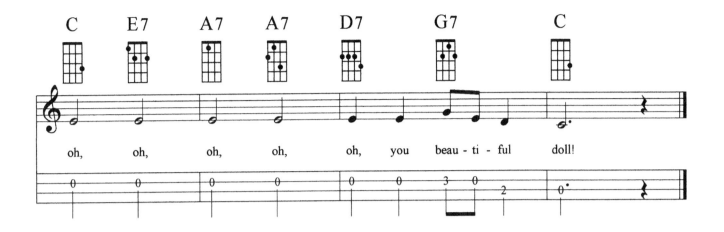

oh,   oh,   oh,   oh,   oh,   you   beau - ti - ful   doll!

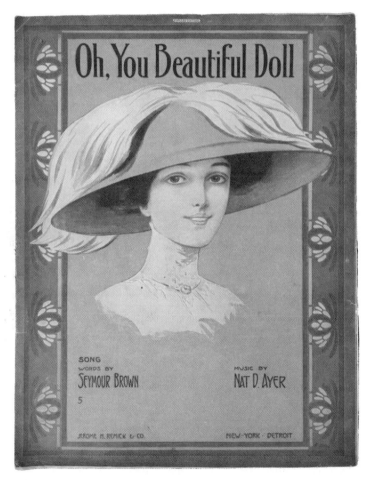

circa 1911

PEG 'O MY HEART

Alfred Bryan

Ukulele in Low G tuning: GCEA

Fred Fisher

C7   F

come be my own,   come make your home in my   heart._____

If you enjoy songs with an Irish flavor be sure to check out Centerstream's *Irish Songs for Ukulele.* Fifty-five favorites of authentic songs and tunes from Ireland as well as a large assortment of Irish-American ballads -- all with great arragements for the ukulele.

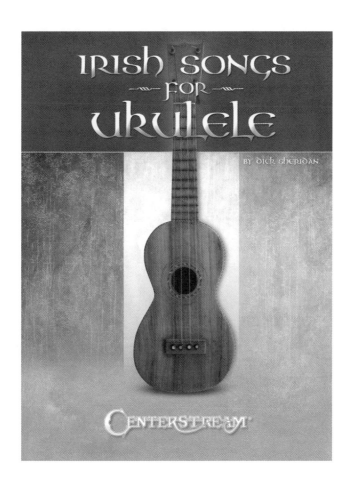

POOR BUTTERFLY

Ukulele in Low G tuning: GCEA

Raymond Hubbell

POOR BUTTERFLY

Inspired by the unrequited love theme of Giacomo Puccini's opera "Madama Butterfly."

ROSE OF WASHINGTON SQUARE

Ballard MacDonald Ukulele in Low G tuning: GCEA James F. Hanley

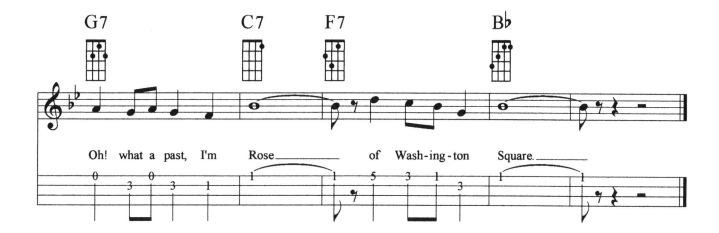

Oh! what a past, I'm Rose_____ of Wash-ing-ton Square._____

JIM JAM JEMS was a popular monthly editorial news magazine published from 1912 to 1929 in Bismark, ND. Mostly text but with occasional cartoons and artwork, it relied on humor, satire, and propaganda for social and political commentray to advance its motto of "A Volley of Truth."

RUBE GOLDBERG (1883-1970) was a cartoonist initially for the *New York Evening News* and later other New York newspapers. He is known for his immaginative cartoons depicting complicated machinery and gadgets that solved simple problems in bizarre ways.

WASHINGTON SQUARE is an iconic neighborhood of New York City located at the south end of Fifth Avenue in Greenwich Village. Its park has long been a center for artists, writers, and activists. The park is dominated by a stone arch 77 feet tall commemorating the centennial of George Washington's presidential innauguration.

ROSE ROOM

Ukulele in Low G tuning: GCEA

Harry Williams

Art Hickham

PLANXTY IRWIN

Ukulele in Low G tuning: GCEA

Traditional Irish

SECOND HAND ROSE

Grant Clarke   Ukulele in Low G tuning: GCEA   James F. Hanley

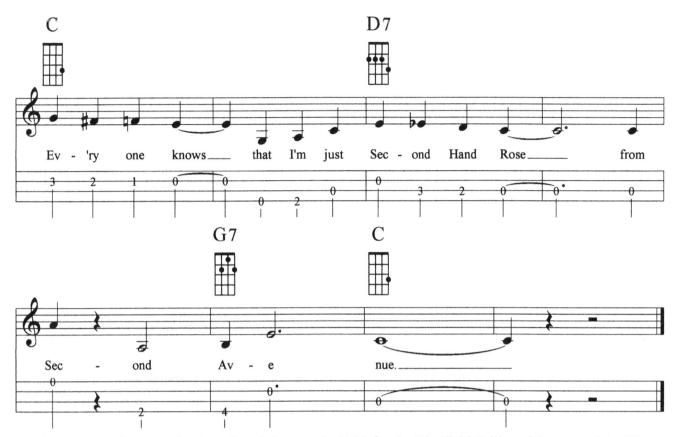

Comedienne Fanny Brice introduced the song in 1921 for the Ziegfield Follies of that year. Her life and career were portrayed by Barbara Streisand in the the 1964 Broadway show "Funny Girl" which was turned into a movie in 1968 with Streisand recapturing the role in her film debut.

Composer James F. Hanley was the father of a childhood friend. Sadly, he passed away when my friend and I were only in the second grade. Although I knew the family well, I unfortunately didn't know my friend's father. I recall seeing him just once, a stout man in a dark suit walking home from the Douglaston railroad station on Long Island.

The Hanley house was a Mediterranean-style structure with a small courtyard in back that led to a garage above which was a large room with a grand piano that apparently had been a studio for Hanley. After his passing, the room fell into disuse and became a playroom for my friend and me. By then it was musty with the floor littered with forgotten manuscript. I've often wondered since what treasures those discarded music sheets might have contained.

Hanley was a pianist who started as an accompanist for valudeville and then went on to creating scores for stage and film including the Ziegfield Follies and George White's Scandals. In addition to *Second Hand Rose* he had several other hits including *Back Home In Indiana, Zing! Went the Strings of My Heart*, and *Rose of Washington Square*. He was inducted posthumously into the Songwriters Hall of Fame in 1970.

See the song *Rose of Washington Square*, also included in this book.

SAY IT WITH MUSIC

Ukulele in Low G tuning: GCEA

Irvng Berlin

THERE'LL BE SOME CHANGES

Billy Higgins

Ukulele in Low G tuning: GCEA

W. Benton Overstreet

THERE'LL BE SOME CHANGES

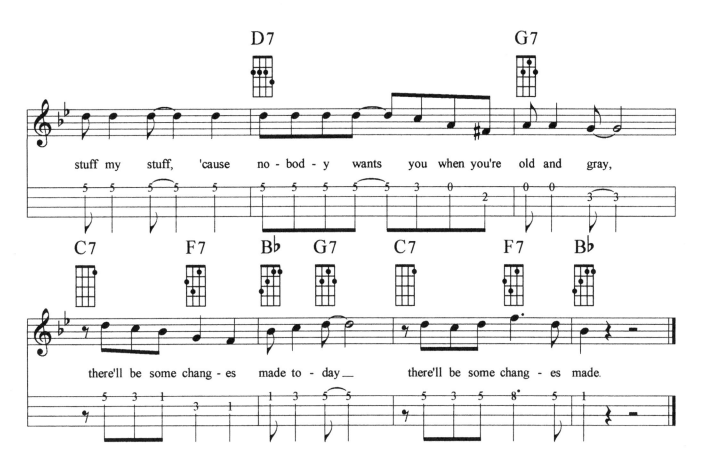

D7 **G7**

stuff my   stuff, 'cause   no - bod - y   wants   you when you're   old and   gray,

C7 **F7** **B♭** **G7** **C7** **F7** **B♭**

there'll be some chang - es   made to - day __   there'll be some chang - es   made.

WAY DOWN YONDER IN NEW ORLEANS

Henry Creamer | Ukulele in Low G tuning: GCEA | John Turner Layton, Jr.

Way down yon-der in New Or - leans in the land of dream-y scenes

there's a gar - den of E - den, that's what I mean,

Cre - ole ba - bies with flash-ing eyes softly whis-per with ten-der sighs,

Stop! oh, won't you give your la - dy fair a lit-tle smile,

YOU MADE ME LOVE YOU

Ukulele in Low G tuning:GCEA

Joseph McCarthy

James V. Monaco

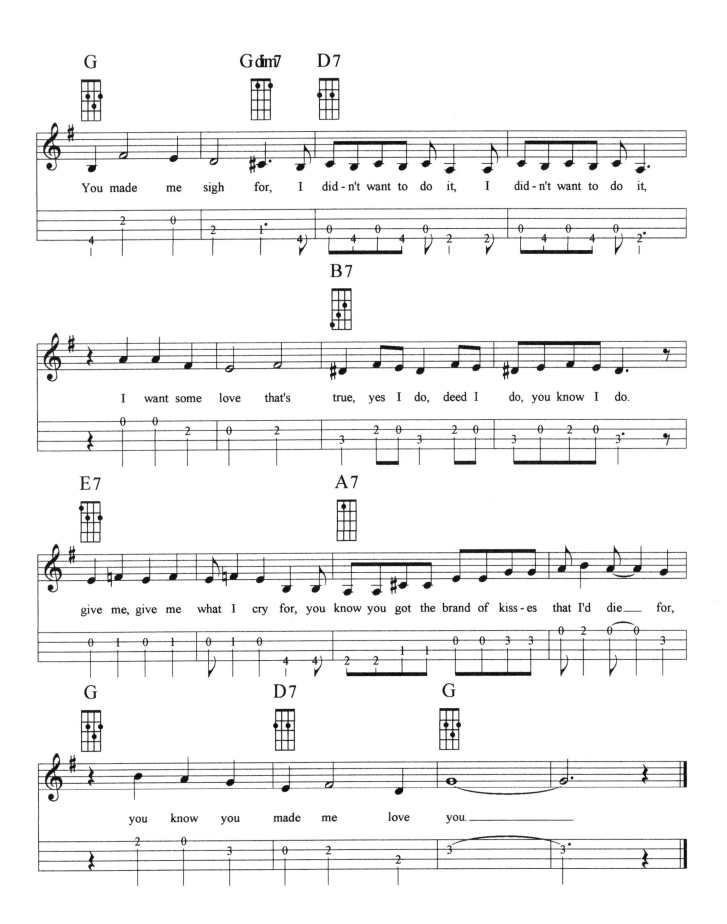

More Great Books from Dick Sheridan...

More Great Ukulele Books from Centerstream...

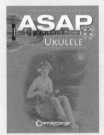